A Stoic's Guide to Human Interaction

Navigating Personal and Professional Relationships

Table of Contents

Chapter 1. Introduction

In this invigorating Special Report, "A Stoic's Guide to Human Interaction: Navigating Personal and Professional Relationships", we break down the ancient wisdom of Stoicism into relatable, practical lessons for the modern citizen. Wouldn't it be wonderful to always enjoy serene poise, regardless of personal and professional tribulations? Flawlessly blending concept and practice, this comprehensive report helps you manifest the spirit of Stoicism in your interactions, aiding you in establishing healthier associations, improving conflict resolution, and ultimately gaining peace of mind. The stoic approach has profound potential to transform not only your emotions and thoughts but also the dynamics of your relationships, fostering resilience in the midst of the unpredictable tide that encompasses human interaction. So, brace yourself for an enlightening journey, full of enriching insights, that will take your interpersonal skills to unmatched heights and blissful tranquility!

Chapter 2. Introduction to Stoicism: Origins and Principles

Stoicism, a practical philosophical movement originating nearly 2300 years ago from Athens, Greece, has been guiding countless generations toward tranquility, depth of understanding, and worthy personal and societal behavior. Evolved from the teachings of Zeno of Citium, Stoicism grew into a robust school of life, advocating for mastery of emotions, virtues, and wisdom, influencing culture, academia, and individual lives profoundly across the world even today.

2.1. Understanding Stoicism

Stoicism is more than just a philosophical concept; it's a lifestyle that encourages embracing one's destiny and the rational comprehension of life, virtue, and relationships. By accepting the world's nature, including its tumult and adversity, we gain emotional resilience and serenity. Fundamentally, Stoicism provides guidance on managing negative emotions and impulses that could potentially disrupt our peace of mind and relationships.

2.2. The Birth of Stoicism

The roots of Stoicism date back to the early 3rd century BC, with Zeno of Citium as its progenitor. An affluent merchant, Zeno experienced a dramatic shipwreck, losing nearly all his wealth. He found solace in philosophy, eventually developing the core principles of Stoicism, which he began teaching at the painted porch, or 'Stoa Poikile' in Athens, giving birth to the term 'Stoicism.'

2.3. Core Principles of Stoicism

Stoicism revolves around four cardinal virtues: wisdom, courage, justice, and temperance. These virtues guide how a Stoic should perceive and react to life's various situations, cornerstone to both personal and professional relationships.

1. Wisdom: It refers to the application of knowledge and good judgment in everyday situations. Stoics relentlessly pursue wisdom by learning, experiencing, and introspecting to deal with life's complexities.

2. Courage: Stoicism encourages assertiveness in confronting adversity. It isn't about fearlessness but handling fear and acting in alignment with morality and reason despite apprehension.

3. Justice: Stoics uphold the principles of fairness, kindness, and community service. Everyone should be treated ethically, and social responsibilities should be fulfilled.

4. Temperance: It embodies practicing restraint, moderation in desires, and achieving a balance in life.

The practice of these virtues helps in developing a clear, unbiased mind, ready to face the pressures of daily life, responding to situations not impulsively but rationally.

2.4. Stoicism & the Dichotomy of Control

Crucial to Stoic philosophy is the dichotomy of control, emphasizing understanding what's within our control and what's not. According to the Stoic philosopher Epictetus, we control our thoughts, behaviors, and choices. Conversely, we lack control over external factors—worldly events or others' thoughts and actions.

Stoics focus energy on what they can influence, accepting the rest with equanimity. This acceptance forms the basis for maintaining tranquility amidst turbulence, necessary for strong, stable relationships.

2.5. The Role of Fate in Stoicism

In Stoicism, much importance is given to acceptance—of oneself, others, and fate. Stoics believe in destiny, accepting what life brings without resentment. This notion, known as 'Amor Fati' or love of fate, implies that everything, be it victory or loss, joy or sorrow, contributes to the grand scheme of life.

It isn't about passive resignation, but actively loving what happens, a powerful approach toward life's unpredictability, essential for sustaining internal peace and fostering healthier relationships.

In conclusion, Stoicism involves cultivating inner virtues, focusing on self-improvement, and accepting the nature of life and the world. As we embark on learning how to apply this philosophy to our interpersonal relationships, remember the words of Seneca, a famous Stoic philosopher: "All the art of living lies in a fine mingling of letting go and holding on." The following chapters are designed to immerse you in the art of Stoic living and bring forth a transformative shift in your personal and professional interactions.

Chapter 3. The Stoic Mindset: Adopting a Purposeful Outlook

Serenity, resilience, philosophical tranquility. These have been associated with the practice of Stoicism. But what propels such virtues to shine? It is the exercise of the 'Stoic Mindset'. Embarking upon this journey requires us to adopt a purposeful perspective.

3.1. The Nature of the Stoic Mindset

Stoicism is no abstract belief system sealed off in ancient manuscripts. It is designed to be lived and breathed in our everyday situations. The foundation of the Stoic mindset lies upon the dichotomy principle – the identification and differentiation between what can be controlled and what cannot. The Stoic mindset postulates that your well-being and tranquility don't hinge upon your external circumstances, but rather on how you interpret, respond, and navigate these circumstances.

Stoicism is not about suppressing emotions or feelings. Instead, it places rationality above the whims of the emotional mind. It's about focusing on our responses, our perceptions, our actions, rather than pining over what is not in our control. This mindset may seem radical at first glance, yet when thoroughly understood, it can precipitate a cascade of liberating realizations and meaningful changes to how you interact with the world.

3.2. Emulation of Sage: Striving for Virtue

At the heart of our purposeful Stoic journey lies the concept of the Sage, the ideal Stoic practitioner free from negative emotions and hasty judgment. The Sage is not a literal person to find but is an aspiration for the Stoic to strive toward. This pursuit of Sagehood suggests that the path to eudaimonia, or true happiness, lies not in the treasures or titles the world has to offer but rather within moral virtues of wisdom, justice, bravery, and self-discipline.

On a practical level, this involves embracing the virtues while also acknowledging your faults and weaknesses. It means dedicating yourself to the pursuit of your highest self, knowing that although you may never perfectly embody the Sage, the act of striving for it has immense value in itself. It is a journey, not a destination. It is a purpose, not an ending.

3.3. The Role of Rationality

Rationality reigns supreme in a Stoic's life. The ability to reason and make logical, impartial decisions is seen as our highest faculty and the most distinguishing feature of being human. It calls for a consciousness rooted in calmness and clarity, uprooting the impulsive decisions that spin us into the whirlpool of regret.

This isn't asserting that we shed away our feelings and sentiments. Stoicism is not the enemy of emotions. Rather, it aspires to strike a balance between emotions and reasoning, ensuring they serve us, not control us. Using our rational mind to process our feelings allows for a more thoughtful interpretation of our experiences, aiding us in making healthier, more beneficial decisions.

3.4. Acceptance of the Uncontrollable: Practicing Amor Fati

The Stoic philosophy upholds acceptance - acknowledging things as they are, rather than how we would like them to be. This acceptance is embodied in the Latin phrase, "Amor Fati" (Love of Fate), where you not only accept everything that happens in life but also learn to love it.

This acceptance doesn't equate to fatalism or resignation; instead, it fosters resilience. It's about understanding that we can't always control what happens in life, but we can manage how we react and perceive it. As often asserted in Stoicism, it's not the event that disturbs us, but our perception of the event.

3.5. Development of Inner Citadel: Awakening Inner Resilience

In wielding the Stoic mindset, we construct what's known as the 'Inner Citadel.' It's our sanctuary of mental tranquility and our fortress against the adversities life tends to hurl at us. The Inner Citadel is symbolic of our inner strength, resilience, and composure.

Cultivating your inner citadel involves practicing mindfulness, developing virtue, nurturing rationality, and exercising acceptance. This stoic fortress is built not overnight, but stone by stone, experience by experience, thought by thought. You'll find that armed with this structured internal fortitude, even when the turbulence of life rages, your mind remains tranquil.

3.6. Stoic Exposure: Beating Fear with Experience

Also fundamental to the Stoic framework is the practice of 'premeditatio malorum', or the premeditation of evils. It encourages envisaging worst-case scenarios to desensitize our fear and apprehension. Rather than fostering negative views, it serves to prepare us mentally, reducing the shock factor while building resilience.

Such Stoic exposure introduces a new lens to view life. It might be arduous initially, yet as practiced frequently, it cultivates strength and emotional stability, reinforcing our ability to handle challenging circumstances.

3.7. Incorporating Nature's Flow: Living According To Nature

Stoicism intones a profound respect for nature and harmony with its flow. Everything in this universe functions through some rationale or logic, and humans, as per Stoic philosophy, are no exception. Living according to nature, in Stoicism, means understanding our true nature as rational and social beings, exercising our reason, and fulfilling our responsibilities towards society.

Such understanding establishes a nurturing relationship with the universe at large, inducing a profound sense of connectivity, reducing feelings of isolation or alienation. It fosters collaborative behavior, paving the way for healthier human interactions.

In essence, the Stoic mindset allows us to comprehend life's trials with wisdom and resilience, rendering us better equipped to navigate the changing tides of our personal and professional situations. Its adoption is a journey, a path towards lasting tranquility and, ultimately, a fulfilled life. The process is an awakening unto itself, propelling us to encounter reality without fear, but with acceptance, understanding, and an open heart.

Chapter 4. Navigating Personal Relationships: Family and Friends Through a Stoic Lens

Understanding family and friends through a Stoic perspective is a journey of introspection and external observation. A harmonious balance between these two facets enables you to implement Stoic wisdom into your interactions with those closest to you, thereby nurturing improved relationships and reducing emotional turmoil.

4.1. Understanding Stoicism

Stoicism, a philosophy originating from ancient Greece, teaches self-control, fortitude, and a sense of empathy to overcome destructive emotions, thus guiding you toward inner peace irrespective of external circumstances. Stoics understand that everything external is ephemeral, uncontrollable, and shouldn't be the source of our happiness or distress. Instead, our reactions and attitudes towards these elements should take center stage in our quest for tranquillity.

4.2. Apply Stoic Principles in Interactions with Family

Family dynamics are diverse and often complicated, but they are a constant and significant part of our lives. Applying Stoicism can streamline interactions, alleviating strife, and cultivating harmony.

4.2.1. The Dichotomy of Control

A key idea in Stoicism is understanding that some things are within our control, while others are not. Concentrate on what you can control — your thoughts, beliefs, and actions, while relinquishing control over others and their actions. Frustration often stems from trying to control the uncontrollable. Accepting this dichotomy helps foster peace in familial relationships.

For example, if a family member frequently arrives late for gatherings, rather than becoming frustrated, choose to adjust your reactions and accept that their timeliness is outside your control.

4.2.2. Practicing Empathy

Stoicism isn't about suppressing emotions, but understanding and managing them. Empathy, a profound understanding of another's feelings, becomes a valuable tool in enhancing family relationships. Realize that each has their battle to fight, bringing patience and understanding to your interactions.

For instance, if a sibling is continually venting their frustrations on you, understand that they might be dealing with considerable stress. Treat them with compassion, but also set healthy boundaries to safeguard your tranquility.

4.3. Implement Stoic Philosophy in Friendships

Friendships, much like familial relationships, can benefit immensely from Stoic principles. Though not bound by blood, these relationships deeply impact our lives and wellbeing.

4.3.1. Value of Virtue

Stoicism places immense accentuation on virtue. Marcus Aurelius, the Roman emperor and stoic philosopher, referred to virtues as our 'good qualities'. The four cardinal virtues in Stoicism are wisdom, courage, justice, and temperance. Foster these virtues in friendships and see them flourish.

For example, demonstrate wisdom by offering thoughtful advice. Exhibit courage during their challenging times. Uphold justice in disagreements. And apply temperance by balancing your needs with those of others.

4.3.2. Friendships and Indifference

Stoics differentiate between 'preferred indifferents' (wealth, health, and friends) and 'unpreferred indifferents' (poverty, sickness, and enemies). The idea is not to shun friendships but to treasure them without becoming dependent on them for happiness.

4.4. Developing Stoic Practices

Consistency is key in manifesting the philosophy of Stoicism. Implement these practices in interactions with family and friends regularly.

4.4.1. Reflective Journaling

A valuable tool in Stoicism is reflective journaling. At the end of each day, write your thoughts and feelings about interactions that day. Ask yourself how you implemented the stoic principles and where you lapsed. It aids in self-awareness and mirrors your progress.

4.4.2. Meditation and Mindfulness

Marcus Aurelius' writings are full of reminders to stay present. Practicing mindfulness helps you be more aware of your reactions, while meditation provides the space to observe your emotions without judgement, hence better equipping you to handle difficult situations.

4.4.3. Continuous Learning

Stoicism is a lifelong journey. Continuously seek knowledge, learn from experience and never cease in your quest to better understand Stoic principles.

In essence, viewing personal relationships through the lens of Stoicism paves the way for stability and fulfillment. It isn't about suppressing emotions or attaining an unfeeling state of nirvana, but about achieving a deep understanding of self, others, and the dynamics of interaction. Stoicism ushers in an era of improved personal relationships characterized by comprehension, acceptance, and peaceful coexistence.

Chapter 5. Professional Relationships: The Stoic Way to Workplace Harmony

Emperors, slaves, and famed thinkers alike relied on one philosophy to govern their daily lives – Stoicism. Born in the heart of a bustling Athens, Stoicism is not merely a set of beliefs but a way of life that upholds the values of virtue, tolerance, and self-discipline. As we pry open the treasures of Stoicism, we can transmute its wisdom into practical strategies to elevate our workplace interactions and fabricate harmonious working relationships.

5.1. Understanding Stoic Philosophy

Before diving into specific strategies, it's crucial to grasp the central premises of Stoicism. Stoic philosophers taught that it wasn't external events or people that distressed us, but rather our reactions and perceptions. They advocated for understanding what is within our control and what isn't, a vital determiner of our emotional wellbeing. By learning to accept what's beyond us and focusing solely on our actions and reactions, we embark on the stoic path.

5.2. Stoicism and Control

Stoic philosophers divided aspects of life into two categories: those that we can control (our thoughts, attitudes, responses) and those we cannot (other people, events, outcomes). This perspective redirects our attention and efforts to our internal landscape, creating room for growth and self-improvement.

Navigating the professional landscape becomes smoother when we accept that many factors are beyond our control: a colleague's attitude, market conditions, or the whims of the economy. These are externals. What we can control, however, is our reactions, interpretations, emotions, and the decisions we make based on these.

5.3. Applying Stoicism In Conflict Resolution

Impartiality, courtesy, responsive communication - these are the tenets of Stoic thought that can be wielded effectively in conflict resolution at work. Stoicism may, in fact, be the underutilized tool to anchoring more open, cooperative, and harmonious workplaces.

Rather than impulsively reacting when emotions run high, take a moment to reflect. Breathe. Remember that your feelings, not the provoking event, determine your well-being. This stoic trait of emotional resilience provides a buffer against knee-jerk reactions, creating space for more informed, thoughtful responses.

5.4. The Stoic Response to Workplace Stress

Stress is ubiquitous in the professional world. Stoicism, by distinguishing the controllable from the uncontrollable, aids in managing stress significantly. Being stoic doesn't equate to being emotionless or indifferent. It means accepting situations, understanding your limitations, and then committing yourself completely to what you can control.

If a project deadline is moved up, for instance, you can choose to worry and let stress consume you, or you can adjust your schedule and workflow realistically, focusing on managing your efforts and time competently.

5.5. Building Effective and Efficient Teams

Stoicism emphasizes empathy and understanding, fostering effective team collaborations. When you react less to the actions of others and focus more on your responses, it nurtures a positive work environment.

Appreciating individual skills and using them to achieve a common goal, without fretting over individual differences or internal squabbles, lays the foundation for progressive teamwork.

5.6. Resilience in Face of Failure and Challenges

How a stoic responds to roadblocks is integral to their philosophy. Instead of seeing challenges as setbacks, Stoicism exhorts us to view them as opportunities for growth and learning. Therein lies the stoic mantra- The obstacle is the way.

When faced with failure, a stoic employee would introspect and gain insights about their performance and areas of improvement, instead of surrendering to despondency or frustration.

5.7. Gratitude and Contentment

Another key aspect of Stoicism involves appreciating what one already has. It encourages the cultivation of gratitude and contentment in the face of capitalism's anxiety-inducing never-ending chase of wealth and status.

This doesn't mean that ambition is wrong. Stoic philosophy merely posits that external possessions or status should not be the sole determiner of happiness or self-worth.

Inculcating gratitude fosters positive workplace relations, reduces stress, and enhances overall life satisfaction.

Through the stoic lens, we can dissect and distill the cyclic turbulence of our professional lives into manageable fragments, ultimately reaching a state of equanimity and harmony. Stoicism empowers us to cater to our well-being while navigating the intricate mazes of our professional lives. Indeed, such is the profound potential of this age-old wisdom - fostering resilience in the unpredictable tide that is human interaction.

Chapter 6. Stoicism and Conflict Resolution: Calming the Storm

As human beings, we are bound to encounter conflicts that arise from diverging interests, misinterpretations, or emotional outbursts. Stoicism, with its rational and empathetic approach, provides a path to navigate these situations efficiently, as it emphasizes the transformation of our perceptions and reactions. The Stoics held an unwavering belief in the power of rational thought, empathy, and control over one's perceptions. Their principles can be leveraged effectively in conflict resolution by cultivating a calm demeanor and driving balanced dialogue.

6.1. The Stoic Virtues in Conflict Resolution

Stoicism promotes four cardinal virtues: wisdom, courage, justice, and temperance. As essentially social beings, it is imperative for us to understand how these virtues can guide us in diffusing confrontations and establishing harmony.

Wisdom is the ability to discern what's truly important in a situation, understand the viewpoints of others, and identify the most effective solution. In conflict scenarios, it's essential to remember to avoid unnecessary confrontations and choose our battles wisely.

Courage in Stoicism is not only about physical bravery but also about moral courage. It encourages us to voice our opinion respectfully, confront uncomfortable truths, and admit our mistakes.

Justice, from a Stoic's viewpoint, involves understanding the situation from a balanced perspective. It demands fairness in proceedings, comprehension of the viewpoints involved, and making impartial decisions.

Temperance calls for self-restraint, keeping our passions in check, and avoiding impulsive reactions. It provides the poise to keep our emotions under control during disagreements.

When effectively integrated in our approach to conflict, these virtues can serve as a lighthouse, illuminating the pathway to resolution and peace.

6.2. Understanding and Controlling Perception

Perception is a primary determinant of how we react to conflicts. Stoicism places a great emphasis on mastering perceptions to regulate emotional responses. The revered Stoic philosopher, Epictetus, once stated, "People are not disturbed by things, but by the view they take of them." Thus, altering our perception of conflicts can dramatically alter our emotional state.

In the face of disagreement, try to perceive it as a learning opportunity rather than seeing it as a personal attack. Understand that human beings are inherently different and will have diverging views. This mindset can defuse the situation and encourage open communication.

6.3. Emotional Intelligence and Empathy

Recognizing one's emotions, understanding others' feelings, and managing emotional responses are critical for conflict resolution. A stoic cultivates emotional intelligence through introspection and empathy.

Remember to pause and introspect. Identify emotions arising within you and question their origins. Engage in metacognition, evaluating whether your thoughts are facts or perceptions. Identify any negative feelings and acknowledge their existence, instead of suppressing or intensifying them. This level of self-awareness aids in better emotional regulation.

Empathy—the capacity to understand another's perspective—is essential for resolving disagreements. Stoics practice empathy not to absorb others' emotions, but to comprehend their viewpoints.

6.4. Communicating Effectively

Effective communication is the bridge that connects differing sides, vital to achieving resolution. Stoic teachings emphasize honesty, clarity, and active listening while communicating.

In conflicts, express your feelings truthfully, maintaining a level-headed disposition. Revise your words for clarity; ambiguous language can often lead to misinterpretations. Active listening fosters understanding. Be attentive to the other party's words, and seek confirmations to ensure you have accurately grasped their standpoint.

6.5. Paving the Path to Resolution

Once you comprehend the prerequisites for efficient conflict management, the final step involves navigating towards resolution. Here, the wisdom of Stoicism is invaluable, as you apply the concepts of compromise, acceptance, and peaceful conflict closure.

Compromise is a two-way street, calling for flexibility from all involved. Align your expectations with the realm of possibility, encouraging an environment where everyone feels heard and respected. In some instances, disagreements may seem unresolvable. It is essential for the stoic mind to accept that conflicts might not always resolve in ways we prefer.

Navigating personal and professional conflicts can be emotionally draining. Yet, through the robust foundations of Stoicism, one can cultivate resilience, establish a rational mind, and move towards a calm resolution. As Marcus Aurelius advised, "You have power over your mind—not outside events. Realize this, and you will find strength." Life, inevitably peppered with conflicts, can become a journey of growth and learning when illuminated with a stoic light.

Chapter 7. The Power of Emotion Control: Stoic Principles in Practice

The Stoics believed that our emotions stem not from external events or individuals, but our perception of them. Before we delve into the practical application of Stoic principles for emotional control, it's quintessential to understand the groundwork laid by the Stoic philosophers.

7.1. The Dichotomy of Control

One of the cornerstones of Stoic philosophy is the dichotomy of control, which instructs us to distinguish between the things we can control – our beliefs, judgments, and actions – and those we cannot – everything outside our own mind.

Often, our emotions are triggered by external events or circumstances. Consider a scenario wherein your supervisor gives a project you were earnestly hoping for to another colleague. Your initial reaction may be one of disappointment, even resentment. According to Stoicism, you can't control your supervisor's decision, but you can control your reaction to it. From a Stoic's stance, it's essential to shift your focus from the uncontrollable circumstance to your controllable response.

7.2. Practicing Objective Representation

Another powerful Stoic principle in controlling emotions is practicing objective representation or seeing things as they are, devoid of our personal biases and unnecessary embellishments.

Consider a situation where your best friend did not invite you to a social gathering. Instead of latching onto feelings of betrayal and exclusion, Stoicism advises us to observe the event objectively. The objective fact is, "You were not invited to the gathering." All negative emotions originate not from this fact but from the narrative you attach to it.

7.3. Understanding Impermanence and Acceptance

Stoicism teaches us to accept things as they are and understand the nature of impermanence. Nothing in life is permanent; change is the only constant. Situations change, relationships evolve, people come in and out of our lives, and all of these can set off a roller-coaster of emotions. However, persistently reminding ourselves about the transient nature of life can help manage our emotional responses.

7.4. The Art of Negative Visualization

Negative visualization is a premeditative practice where we regularly contemplate potential negative events or losses. This practice doesn't foster pessimism but prepares you for adversity, alleviating the emotional distress in case the anticipated circumstance occurs.

Now that we have established the foundational Stoic principles let's explore practical approaches for integrating these in daily life.

7.5. Daily Practice: Journaling

Journaling is an effective way to sift through emotions and thoughts, providing clarity. Begin by noting down the emotional responses towards the day's events and then examine these reactions under the lens of Stoic principles.

7.6. Mindful Meditation

The practice of mindful meditation trains your mind to remain present, allowing a vantage point to observe your responses and emotions objectively. As you become more aware of your emotional landscape, you will find gradual ease in disentangling from negative emotional responses.

7.7. Mental Simulations

Mental simulations using negative visualization can be a potent tool to anticipate and prepare for adversities. Regular practice can inoculate you against emotional upheaval when these anticipated negatives occur.

Remember, Stoicism is more than ancient wisdom; it is a philosophy of life. Embracing Stoic principles in everyday life calls for continuous practice and perseverance. The road might seem arduous at times, but by persisting, you will attain a heightened sense of emotional control, leading to tranquility and resilience in the face of adversities. So, step forth and begin your fascinating journey of emotional wisdom with Stoicism!

Chapter 8. Resilience Building: Stoicism's Key to Weathering Life's Storms

The tempestuous journey of life is a complex tapestry of trials and triumphs, woven by the warp and weft of external circumstances and our internal responses to them. Stoicism, an ancient philosophy that has stood the test of time, prescribes a resilient approach to confronted adversities. Emulating the indifference of a boulder to the passing storm, stoics build a fortress of resilience that houses peace and tranquility amid the swirl of life's volatile weather.

8.1. Stoicism and Resilience: An Inseparable Bond

In the Stoic understanding of resilience, hardships aren't seen as external events that befall us, but as opportunities to exercise virtue and to strengthen character. The principle lies in the perception of situations. A challenging event only gains the power to disturb us if we permit it. If it's viewed as an opportunity for personal growth and moral development, it loses its potency to instill fear or worry.

Epictetus, a renowned Stoic philosopher, famously posited, "It's not things that upset us, but our judgments about things." This perspective emboldens us to reframe our understanding of adversity and fortify our mental resilience. Instead of allowing external happenings to dictate our emotional state, we can choose a balanced and composed response, executing control over the only thing truly within our command - our perceptions and reactions.

Marcus Aurelius, a practicing Stoic and Roman Emperor, penned down thoughtful expressions about resilience in his seminal work,

'Meditations'. He wrote, "You have power over your mind, not outside events. Realize this, and you will find strength." Here, resilience isn't about eliminating adversity but understanding and accepting its inevitable presence, responding with fortitude while staying detached from the supposed calamity.

8.2. Stoic Practices to Build Resilience

Table 1. Stoic Techniques for Resilience-Building

Stoic Practice	Description
Negative Visualization	Regularly envisioning worst-case scenarios helps in building mental resilience, preparing us for the potential upheavals of life.
Dichotomy of Control	Understanding what is under our control helps in managing our reactions and action. This knowledge wards off unease and helps us maintain tranquility.
Premeditatio Malorum	This practice of foreseeing potential setbacks enables us to avoid shock, remain composed when pitfalls occur, and encourages proactive problem-solving.

Stoic Practice	Description
Practicing Good Character	Virtue, according to Stoics, is the highest good. Cultivating virtues like courage, wisdom, justice, and moderation builds resilience, equipping us to face trials honorably.
Self-denial	Regularly exposing ourselves to discomfort builds tolerance, reducing our sensitivity to hardship, and promoting resilience.

8.3. Embracing Adversity: A Lesson in Resilience

To build resilience, according to Stoics, we must re-imagine adversity as a tool for character development and not as an undesirable villain. Every challenge faced is an invitation to become stronger, wiser, and more virtuous; offering a chance to practice Stoic principles, like wisdom, courage or duty.

Adopting this view reframes adversity from a dreaded foe to an esteemed trainer, refining and fortifying our character. Even if the adversity seems overwhelming and resistant to control, Stoics contend that we can still govern our response, adhering to virtue and preserving tranquility.

Consider the example of James Stockdale who, during the Vietnam War, applied Stoic principles to endure seven and a half years as a prisoner of war. His steadfast belief in Stoic philosophy, particularly Epictetus's teachings, fortified him to stand firm against severe trials.

8.4. Cultivating Virtues to Fortify Resilience

Stoics assign paramount importance to the cultivation of virtues. Four cardinal virtues form the pillar of Stoic philosophy: Wisdom, Courage, Justice, and Temperance.

- Wisdom impacts resilience through the discernment of what is within our control and what is not. This clear understanding helps us absorb the shock of adversity and respond optimally.

- Courage emboldens us not only to face adversity head-on but also to exercise wisdom consistently, upholding sound judgement when surrounded by turmoil.

- Justice guides our interactions, ensuring that even during crises, we respond with fairness. This equable approach fosters harmonious relationships and effectively mitigates conflict.

- Temperance or moderation promotes a balanced response to adversity, tempering extreme reactions or overreactions that could lead to stress or regret.

A proper grasp and diligent cultivation of these virtues contribute substantially to the strengthening of individual and collective resilience.

8.5. Resilience in Action: Stoicism for Modern Life

In conclusion, the tenets of stoicism promote resilience and peace amid life's tumult. This pragmatic philosophy guides us to embrace adversity as an ally, challenging us to learn, grow, and ultimately cultivate mental resilience. It encourages us to maintain equanimity and to act virtuously, grounding us amidst the maelstrom of life's challenges. Moreover, it reframes disturbances from horrendous tormentors to effective trainers, creating a frame that primes resilience and grit.

Stoicism empowers us to weather storms with serenity, to maintain our poise amidst chaos, and to cultivate enduring resilience through the arduous path of life. In the immortal words of the philosopher Seneca, "A gem cannot be polished without friction, nor a man perfected without trials." May we continually strive to realize this Stoic wisdom inline with our interpersonal dynamics, to fortify ourselves against adversity and to strengthen the resilience needed for life's unpredictable tide.

Chapter 9. The Art of Letting Go: Embracing Tranquility and Inner Peace

Stoicism offers a wealth of wisdom in maintaining tranquility and embracing inner peace, especially in regard to letting go of external circumstances beyond our control. This philosophy emphasizes not only the affirmation of life and acceptance of its circumstances but also the dismissal of unnecessary disturbances and conflicts that may cloud our minds.

9.1. Understanding Control

The core principle of Stoicism lies in recognizing and acknowledging what is within our control and what isn't. So often we find ourselves entangled in a web of stress and discontentment, presented by circumstances that fall beyond our reach. Recognize that the things we can control are our own actions, reactions, and opinions. On the contrary, things we cannot control are external circumstances, such as other's actions, natural events, or the past and future.

This is not an invitation to apathy or surrender, rather an encouragement to direct our efforts and energy more efficiently where they will make a positive difference. By doing so, we can diminish a significant amount of unnecessary stress and elevate our sense of inner tranquility.

9.2. Embracing Acceptance

Equanimity lies in accepting life as it unfolds, not as we wish it would. Stoicism advises to resist the human instinct to retaliate against unpleasant occurrences, which only serve to disrupt our inner peace. Instead, we must strive to accept these events as they are and approach them with thoughtfulness and rationality.

We can practice acceptance by taking small steps. When life presents a challenging situation, pause and remind yourself that it's an opportunity for growth, learning, or character-building. By doing so, you can transform adversity into tranquility.

9.3. Practice of Negative Visualization

Stoicism introduces the practice of 'premeditatio malorum', or negative visualization, which involves pondering on potential undesirable outcomes. Whilst this may seem contradictory to the pursuit of tranquility, it serves to prepare us for life's inevitable adversities.

Practicing negative visualization helps us become emotionally resilient when facing actual hardships, and it also enhances our ability to appreciate what we currently have, especially the things we often take for granted. This results in a richer, more joyful, and tranquil existence.

9.4. Detachment: The Path to Freedom

Prospective peace hinges upon our ability to create a healthy detachment from external things and outcomes. Stoicism is firm on the idea that assigning undue importance to external circumstances will only ensnare us in emotional discomfort.

Detachment, however, does not imply that we should stop caring or withdraw from life. Rather, it means developing an internal contentment independent of external conditions. Understand that when we chase after, grasp for, or become overly attached to external entities, peace becomes elusive.

9.5. Discarding Unnecessary Desires

An essential element to gaining tranquility and peace is in discarding unnecessary desires. Stoicism espouses the concept of a minimalistic lifestyle, not just in terms of materialistic possessions, but also in terms of our emotional and mental lives.

By reducing our desires and making peace with simplicity, we can eliminate turmoil that results from wanting more than we need. Pursuing unnecessary aspirations leads to emotional upheaval, which disrupts tranquility. Therefore, simplifying our desires helps to cultivate a calm, content, and serene mind.

9.6. Embodying Resilience

Life's storms are inevitable, and resilience is our only sail. Stoic philosophy encourages the cultivation of resilience to weather any hardship that life throws our way.

Resilience can be nurtured in many ways, such as maintaining a healthy lifestyle, seeking social support, developing emotional intelligence, and adopting a positive mindset. Stoicism provides a sturdy base to build resilience, encouraging us to view adversity as an opportunity for personal growth rather than seeing it as an unfortunate event.

9.7. Reflect to Rectify

Reflection is a powerful tool to achieve peace and tranquility. Stoicism emphasizes self-reflection as crucial for personal improvement.

When you routinely reflect on your thoughts, actions, and reactions, you can better understand yourself, identifying patterns and behaviors that serve or hamper inner tranquility. Armed with this knowledge, you can then make the necessary changes towards maintaining inner peace and life satisfaction.

By combining these stoic practices, you not only learn the art of letting go but also gain the ability to nurture tranquility and inner peace. The path to tranquility may not always be easy, but it is always within reach for those willing to journey it. Through patience, commitment, and practice, you can achieve serenity, regardless of the external circumstances that come your way.

Chapter 10. Stoicism in Everyday Life: From Personal Reflection to Social Interaction

The realm of human interaction is expansive, layered, and, at times, confusing. It is strewn with uncertainties, emotions, implicit expectations, and the unknown perceptions of others, which often affect our emotions and behaviours. Embracing the Stoic philosophy can be transformative in navigating this complex, unpredictable landscape. It promotes rationality and virtuous living, guiding us to peace, prosperity, and pleasure in our personal and professional lives.

10.1. Identifying and Aligning with Your Core Values

The first step towards embodying Stoicism in daily life involves identifying an immutable internal compass - your guiding virtues. Stoics held four primary virtues: wisdom, courage, justice, and temperance. Wisdom is the understanding that some things are within our control - our own opinions and actions - while others, like the opinions, actions, or feelings of others, are not. Courage is having the will to confront fear, pain, and discomfort, especially in sustaining right action. Justice is treating every human being with equity, irrespective of our external differences. Temperance is the exercise of self-restraint and moderation, keeping our desires and impulses in check.

Spend some time in introspection, identifying the virtues that resonate with you. Once identified, aim to align your thoughts, actions, and interactions with these virtues. You'll find situations and people easier to navigate when you have a well-defined internal compass guiding you.

10.2. Practicing Mindful Reflection

Mindful reflection is a crucial tool for Stoics. Practice meditative journaling at the end of each day, reflecting on your experiences, choices, and reactions. Did someone's comment agitate you? Was there a heated argument you wish had gone differently? Write these down, then revisit your core virtues. Reflect on where you strayed from them and how you can realign. This practice fosters self-improvement, tranquility, and a Stoic approach to interactions.

10.3. Dealing with Negative Emotions

In the depths of stressful encounters, negative emotions like anger, irritation, or distress often hijack our responses. Stoics taught an essential antidote - the dichotomy of control. Grasp that some things lie beyond our control, and suffering comes from inappropriately desiring these things to be different. When negative emotions surface, pause, recognize their origins, understand that others' behaviors are beyond your control, then let the negative emotion subside. With practice, this technique promotes emotional stability, happiness, and successful social interaction.

10.4. Fostering Harmonious Relationships

In professional or personal ties, Stoicism steers us towards harmonious relationships based on respect, understanding, and compassion. Remember the virtue of justice - treating others equitably and with dignity. Understand their perspectives and feelings, avoiding premature judgments. Practice active listening, making others feel valued and heard. Express your thoughts calmly and with precise language to prevent miscommunications. When conflicts arise, integrate the Stoic tenets - remember the dichotomy of control, return to your core virtues, and resolve the issue with understanding and calmness.

10.5. Embracing Change and Uncertainty

The only certain thing in life, they say, is uncertainty. One's professional or social environment might drastically change, bringing setbacks or challenges. From the Stoic perspective, accept change as a natural order of the world and an opportunity for growth. Cultivate resilience by reframing negatives into positives - have a growth mindset, viewing obstacles as opportunities for development.

10.6. Resilience to External Opinions

The Stoics believed in an unshakeable 'inner citadel', immune to external opinions. People's perceptions and comments about you can't harm you unless you allow them to. When faced with criticism (constructive or destructive), distil helpful insights for self-improvement, then dismiss the rest as irrelevant. Don't cling to praise either - it creates dependency on the validation of others, which Stoicism teaches to avoid.

Ultimately, the heritage of Stoicism equips us with a magnifying lens to sift through the chaos and unpredictability of day-to-day human interaction. The Stoic tools of aligning with core virtues, mindful reflection, managing emotions, fostering harmonious relationships, embracing change, and developing resilience form a robust framework for thriving in our personal and professional lives. Although this transformation may not happen overnight, steadily practicing and refining these skills will invigorate your journey towards inner tranquility, personal growth, and joyous and serene interactions with the world.

Chapter 11. Epilogue: Transformative Stories of Stoicism in Human Interaction

In the narratives that follow, we delve into the transformative stories of individuals who have applied Stoic principles in their interactions and relationships. Each account illuminates the profound impacts of Stoicism on their emotional states, conflict resolution tactics, and overall quality of their relationships. As these tales unfold, you'll ascertain the remarkable potential of Stoicism to bring about lasting changes and a serene state of mind amidst interpersonal complexities. Be prepared to discover nuggets of profound wisdom hidden in these narratives.

11.1. The Stoic Corporate Ladder Climber

It was during the onset of Jack's career when he landed his first job at a multinational entity that he was introduced to the stoic philosophy. Amid the fierce competitiveness and workplace politics, Jack found himself often daunted, his emotions frequently swinging between stress, frustration, and disillusionment.

Implementing the principles of Stoicism allowed Jack to see his work environment from a new perspective. He learned to differentiate between elements within and beyond his control at work. Trivial conflicts and comments stopped bothering him. He committed to his tasks, focusing solely on his efforts rather than the outcomes. Moreover, he approached confrontations with a calm demeanor, choosing not to retaliate when targeted. Over time, his colleagues, noticing his unwavering tranquility amidst chaos, found themselves drawn to his resilience.

Ultimately, Jack climbed the corporate ranks swiftly, not due to any political maneuvering, but because of his unwavering commitment to his work and the unheard-of tranquility he demonstrated, making him an exceptional leader. His personal transformation also induced changes within the work environment, creating a more empathetic and supportive ambience.

11.2. Family Bonds Strengthened by Stoic Philosophy

Consider Jennifer, a single mother raising two spirited teenagers, facing the classic parental challenges intensified by her solo role. Struggling with fluctuating emotions and frequent conflicts, Jennifer felt overwhelmed until she encountered the life-changing principles of Stoicism.

Intrigued by its promise of maintaining inner tranquility, Jennifer began implementing Stoicism in her familial interactions. It helped her cultivate empathy for her children's adolescent struggles, separating the challenging behaviors from the individuals themselves. She also adopted the stoic principle of not attempting to control what could not be commanded - specifically, her teenagers' choices.

Navigating family dynamics under the stoic lens led to fewer conflicts and deeper connections. Jennifer's children started to appreciate their mother's renewed approach to parenting, fostering a household imbued with understanding and acceptance.

11.3. Amicable Separation: Stoicism Amidst Breakup

Finally, meet Alex, going through a rather messy breakup, dealing with intense emotions and stressful negotiations. He found solace in the pages of Stoic philosophy, where he learned to maintain his composure even whilst navigating the rough waters of a heart-wrenching separation.

He focused on the principles of accepting circumstances as they unfolded and understanding the limits of his control. Instead of resorting to blame games, Alex chose to manage his reactions to his partner's words and actions. He acknowledged his emotions, yet refrained from letting anger and bitterness cloud his judgments or discussions.

The calming influence of Stoic philosophy allowed Alex to process the circumstances with equanimity. The couple managed their breakup proceedings in a relatively amicable manner, minimizing potential harm to their respective mental health and their shared responsibilities.

Through each of these tales, we uncover anecdotal evidence of the transformative influence Stoicism holds over human interaction. Can stoic application ensure the absence of conflict or misunderstandings? Probably not. However, what it assures is the ability to surf these chaotic waves with an unflustered mind and a resilient heart. In embracing Stoicism's timeless wisdom, you too can navigate your personal and professional relationships with a newfound grace, creating ripples of positive change in your interpersonal universe.